Wild Life LOL!™

Giant Pandas

This book is PAND-tastic!

■SCHOLASTIC

Library of Congress Cataloging-in-Publication Data
Names: Children's Press (New York, N.Y.), publisher.
Title: Giant pandas.
Description: New York: Children's Press, an imprint of Scholastic Inc., 2020. | Series: Wild life LOL! | "Produced by Spooky Cheetah Press." | Includes index. | Audience: Grades 2-3 (provided by Children's Press)
Identifiers: LCCN 2019027477 | ISBN 9780531129807 (library binding) | ISBN 9780531132678 (paperback)
Subjects: LCSH: Giant panda—Juvenile literature.
Classification: LCC QL737.C214 G523 2020 | DDC 599.789—dc23 LC record available at https://lccn.loc.gov/2019027477

Produced by Spooky Cheetah Press

Book design by Kimberly Shake. Original series design by Anna Tunick Tabachnik.

Contributing Editor and Jokester: Pamela Chanko

Printed in Heshan, China 62

SCHOLASTIC, CHILDREN'S PRESS, WILD LIFE LOL!™, and associated logos are trademarks and/or registered trademarks of Scholastic Inc.

1 2 3 4 5 6 7 8 9 10 R 29 28 27 26 25 24 23 22 21 20

Scholastic Inc., 557 Broadway, New York, NY 10012.

Photographs ©: cover, spine: Morakot Kawinchan/Shutterstock; cover speech bubbles and throughout: Astarina/Shutterstock; cover speech bubbles and throughout: pijama61/Getty Images; back cover: GlobalP/iStockphoto; 1: GlobalP/iStockphoto; 2: Eric Isselee/Shutterstock; 3 top: Katherine Feng/Minden Pictures; 3 bottom: GlobalP/iStockphoto; 4: Ingo Arndt/Minden Pictures; 5 left: All-Silhouettes.com; 5 right: Denis Sarbashev/Shutterstock; 6-7: Fuse/Getty Images; 8-9: Juan Carlos Muñoz/age fotostock; 10-11: Will Burrard-Lucas/Minden Pictures; 12: mrbfaust/iStockphoto; 13 top left: ronnayut_to/Shutterstock; 13 top right: pzAxe/Shutterstock; 13 bottom left: Jiggo_Putter Studio/Shutterstock; 13 bottom right: phototrip/Alamy Images; 14: Dizzizzmee/Dreamstime; 15 left: ARCO/F Poelking/age fotostock; 15 right: Quirky China/Shutterstock; 16-17: Katherine Feng/Minden Pictures/age fotostock; 18: Katherine Feng/Minden Pictures; 19 left: Mitsuaki Iwago/Minden Pictures; 19 right: Suzi Eszterhas/Minden Pictures; 20-21: Steve Bloom Images/Alamy Images; 22: XINHUA/SIPA/Newscom; 23 left: Ami Vitale/National Geographic Creative; 23 right: Quirky China News/Splash News/Newscom; 24-25: Roman Uchytel/Prehistoric Fauna; 25 bottom right: Eric Isselee/Shutterstock; 26 left: Li Wenbin/VCG/Getty Images; 26 right: Mario Hagen/Shutterstock; 27 left: Johannes Eisele/AFP/Getty Images; 27 right: Keren Su/China Span/Alamy Images; 28 left: Natalia Volkova/Dreamstime; 28 top right: Martin Mecnarowski/Shutterstock; 28 bottom right: wrangel/iStockphoto; 29 left: anankkml/iStockphoto; 29 right: Christian Musat/Shutterstock; 29 bottom: Eric Isselee/Shutterstock; 30 map: Jim McMahon/Mapman ®; 30 inset: Fuse/Getty Images; 31 top: Eric Isselee/Shutterstock; 31 bottom: GlobalP/iStockphoto; 32: GlobalP/iStockphoto.

TABLE OF CONTENTS

MEET THE PLAYFUL PANDA

Are you ready to be amazed and amused? Keep reading. This book will make you flip!

Hi! Wanna play?

LOL!
How do pandas send letters?
BEAR mail!

At a Glance

Where do they live? → Giant pandas live in cool, rainy mountain forests in China.

What do they do? → Giant pandas mostly live alone. They spend most days eating and sleeping.

What do they eat? → Giant pandas mainly eat bamboo.

What do they look like? → Giant pandas have powerful bodies covered in thick black-and-white fur.

How big are they? →

HINT: They're bigger than you. Check this out!

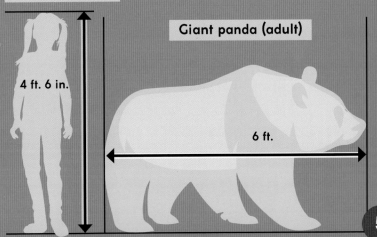

Human (age 9)

4 ft. 6 in.

Giant panda (adult)

6 ft.

PANDA PARADISE

Giant pandas live in the wild in remote mountains of China.

A Cool Home

Pandas live in cool, rainy forests. In winter, this **habitat** is cold and snowy.

In the Neighborhood

The area where a giant panda lives is called its home range. The size of the range depends on how much food is available.

WACKY FACT: Pandas are expert tree climbers and good swimmers.

habitat: any place where a plant or an animal makes its home

The Wanderer
A giant panda may nap in a different cave or tree every day.

Going Solo
Giant pandas mostly live alone except when they are **mating** or when a female is raising her young.

mating: joining together to have babies

A PANDA'S BODY

Pandas are pretty special. There is no mistaking them for another animal.

A Waterproof Coat
A panda's thick, oily fur is waterproof. It also keeps the bear warm during cold winters.

Taking a Shortcut
A panda's short, thick legs allow it to travel close to the ground through dense forests.

One Bear, Two Colors
A panda's black-and-white fur may help it stay hidden among sunlight, shadows, rocks, and snow.

LOL!
What is as big as a panda but weighs nothing?
A panda's shadow!

Just the Right Size
Pandas are not very tall, but they are big. Males can weigh up to 300 pounds. Females are slightly smaller.

PANDA PATTER

Is this panda doing a handstand? Yes! The bear is also leaving a message on the tree.

Ways to Talk
Giant pandas **communicate** with one another through sounds and scents.

So Much to Say
Pandas communicate with 11 different calls. They chirp, bark, honk, chomp, and squeal!

THAT'S EXTREME!
A panda can detect another's scent up to 18 miles away!

Scent-Sational
The animals leave their scent on tree trunks, rocks, bamboo, and bushes to mark their area or attract a mate.

Good Baaaa
Pandas sound like sheep bleating when they greet each other. They may growl when they are angry!

communicate: to share information

A SIMPLE DIET

A giant panda's diet is up to 99 percent bamboo. It is not very nutritious. Pandas need A LOT of it to meet their energy needs. Once in a while pandas eat grass, insects, or fish.

THAT'S EXTREME!
Pandas eat from 23 to 36 pounds of bamboo a day. That would be like you eating 23 to 36 heads of lettuce!

WACKY FACT:
Pandas spend 12 or more hours a day eating!

Waiter, more bamboo, please!

bamboo shoots

bamboo stems

A panda's diet is not very varied.

bamboo leaves

fish

STARTING A FAMILY

A panda is ready to mate at four to eight years old.

1

LOL!
How do pandas say "I like you"?
With a BEAR hug!

FAST FACT:
Female pandas give birth every two to three years.

Scent Marks the Spot

Panda mating season is in spring. To attract a partner, a female makes calls and marks trees with her special scent.

Any day now. . .

Meet Your Mate

After mating, the female panda is pregnant for three to five months. The male panda has gone off on his own.

Ready for Baby

The female panda finds a warm, safe **den** in which to give birth. It may be in the base of a hollow tree or in a cave.

den: the home of a wild animal

SPECIAL DELIVERY

Newborn pandas need lots of care. The mama bear carries her baby gently in her mouth.

Itty-Bitty Baby

Newborn pandas, called cubs, are tiny. They measure about 6 inches long and weigh just 3 to 5 ounces.

THAT'S EXTREME!
A mother panda is 900 times as large as her newborn! A human mom is only about 20 times as big as her baby!

Tickled Pink

Newborn pandas are born pink and hairless. When the baby is a week old, patches of black fur begin to show up.

Peekaboo
A panda can't see when it is first born. The cub finally opens its eyes when it is six to eight weeks old.

WACKY FACT:
A newborn panda is about the size of a stick of butter!

GROWING UP PANDA

Cubs grow fast! Their mom takes care of them and teaches them everything they need to know.

1

LOL!
What does a panda use in the shower?
BEAR-conditioner!

Rock-a-Bye Baby

Pandas are **mammals**, so a cub's first food is its mother's milk. The mother panda gently cradles her tiny cub. She has to be careful not to crush it!

mammals: animals that produce milk to feed their young

THAT'S EXTREME!
A panda cub is ready to climb a tree at six months old.

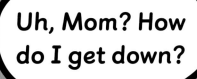

Uh, Mom? How do I get down?

2

3

Baby Steps

The cub spends its first two months inside the den. Then it begins to crawl and can go outside. By the time it is three months old, the cub takes wobbly steps.

Panda School

By the time the cub is six months old, it is ready to explore with its mother and do what she does. The cub still drinks its mother's milk, but it also starts to chew bamboo.

FAMILY LIFE

Panda cubs learn fast how to take care of themselves.

Brrr. Good thing we're wearing fur coats!

LOL!
How did the panda cub get away with her brother's snack?
She BAMBOO-zled him!

FAST FACT:
Panda cubs are curious and playful. They love to roll in the grass and climb on their mother.

1

Crunch Time!

At around nine months old, the cubs are ready to stop drinking their mom's milk. They will eat the same foods their mother eats.

2

Growing Fast

At about one year old, the cub will weigh around as much as an eight-year-old human child: 90 pounds.

3

Bye-Bye, Baby

The young panda stays with its mother until it is about two years old. By then, the panda is independent and can live by itself.

PEOPLE HELPING PANDAS

China is home to panda **breeding** centers, where scientists help raise cubs. This helps the wild panda population grow.

FAST FACT:
Giant pandas in the wild can live up to 20 years. The oldest panda living in captivity survived almost 40 years!

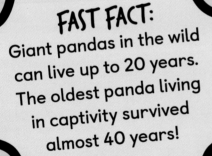

Scientists help
the panda moms have babies. More cubs survive in **captivity** than in the wild.

breeding: helping animals produce offspring

THAT'S EXTREME! About 300 giant pandas live under human care.

WACKY FACT: Scientists soak their suits in panda urine. That way the cubs don't pick up the humans' scent!

Caretakers help

the cubs grow big and strong. But the cubs will need to learn to survive on their own.

Scientists help

by dressing like pandas so the bears don't get used to humans. When the pandas are ready, they're released into the wild.

captivity: living under human care

ANCIENT PANDAS

WACKY FACT: Scientists used to think giant pandas were part of the raccoon family!

Today's pandas look a lot like their ancient **ancestor**. Check it out! Its scientific name is *Kretzoiarctos beatrix*.

Great-Great Grandpa
This animal is the oldest known relative of giant pandas. It lived about 11 million years ago. Scientists found **fossils** in what is now Spain.

Small Fry
K. beatrix weighed about 130 pounds. Modern pandas are almost three times as heavy.

ancestor: a family member who lived long ago

24

Close Relations
Scientists think *K. beatrix* was a lot like modern pandas. It probably fed on tough plants and was a good climber.

LOL!
What do you call an old bear that has lost its teeth?
A gummy bear!

Hola!

You look BEAR-y familiar!

fossils: plants or animals from millions of years ago preserved as rock

PANDAS AND PEOPLE

We have a long history together!

Pre-1960s

1970s

People hunted pandas for their unique black-and-white **pelts**. After years of overhunting, the animals became **endangered**.

Experts estimated that 1,100 pandas were left in the wild. The Chinese government set aside land for panda reserves.

pelts: animal skins with the hair or fur still on

FAST FACT:
In China, one name for the panda is *xióng māo*. That means "bear cat." Some people think the panda has a round face like a cat's!

1989

The Chinese government began taking steps to protect giant panda habitats and to stop the illegal hunting of pandas.

Today

Almost 2,000 pandas can be found in the wild. More than two-thirds of them live in China's 67 protected reserves.

endangered: at risk of dying out

Panda Cousins

Giant pandas are part of the bear family.

We are not big on bamboo—we mainly eat termites and ants.

sloth bears

We are the coolest of all the panda cousins.

We get our name from the golden patch of fur on our chests.

polar bears

sun bears

Please note: Animals are not shown to scale.

The Wild Life

Look at this map of the world. The area in red shows where giant pandas live today: small areas in China. We want giant pandas to continue having habitats to live in. Otherwise, one day there might not be any red left on this map.

Central China

conservation: the protection of nature (like forests and animals)

Protecting Pandas

A lot of people have worked to save pandas. And it's paying off. But even as giant pandas slowly make a comeback, scientists say there is still a lot of work to be done.

Protecting the habitat of giant pandas also helps other animals that share the land, such as the Asiatic black bear, red panda, and leopard cat. Many people—including kids who raise awareness—continue to do their part to ensure the survival of these beautiful bears.

What Can You Do?

You can "adopt" a panda through **conservation** organizations. The money you donate for the adoption is used to protect pandas in the wild. Ask a trusted adult to help you research these groups online. Find creative ways to give money to your favorite organization. You can collect and recycle cans and bottles or have a bake sale.

INDEX

ABOUT THIS BOOK

This book is a laugh-out-loud early-grade adaptation of *Giant Pandas* by Lisa M. Herrington. *Giant Pandas* was originally published by Scholastic as part of its Nature's Children series in 2019.

Saying good-bye is un-BEAR-able!